MOTHERHOOD
OF GOD

*A Report by a Study Group appointed
by the Woman's Guild and the Panel
on Doctrine on the invitation of
the General Assembly of the Church
of Scotland*

Edited by Alan E. Lewis

THE SAINT ANDREW PRESS
EDINBURGH

Published on behalf of
the Woman's Guild/Panel on Doctrine
by THE SAINT ANDREW PRESS
121 George Street, Edinburgh

ISBN 0 7152 0577 3

20028317

231.1

Printed in Great Britain by
Blackwood Pillans & Wilson, Edinburgh

CONTENTS

List of Members of Study Group   iv

Preface   v

1. Introduction   1
   Origin, Conduct and Goal of the Study

2. Background   7
   Seeing the Context

3. A Crucial Issue   13
   Language and God

4. Re-affirming the Tradition   17
   The Fatherhood of God

5. Complementing the Tradition   31
   The Motherly Father

6. Provisional Assessment   47
   Agreement and Controversy

7. The Motherly Father in History   51
   A Devotional Legacy

8. Conclusions   69
   Discrimination and Opportunity

Appendices   69

MEMBERS OF THE WOMAN'S GUILD/PANEL ON DOCTRINE STUDY GROUP

Woman's Guild

1. Mrs. Anne Hepburn, M.A., Convener — National President of the Woman's Guild
2. Mrs. Ann Allen, M.A. — Woman's Guild Branch President
3. Mrs. Dorothy Dalgliesh — Former National Vice-President of the Woman's Guild
4. Mrs. Clara Macrae, B.A., S.Th., Dip.Ed. — Former member of Woman's Guild Central Executive
5. Mrs. Daphne MacNab, M.A. — Former National President of the Woman's Guild
6. Mrs. Jean Morrison, D.C.S. — Former Group Relations Adviser to the Church of Scotland's Education Department

Panel on Doctrine

7. Rev. Dr. John C.L. Gibson, M.A., B.D., D.Phil. — Reader and Head of Department of Hebrew and Old Testament Studies, New College, Edinburgh
8. Rev. Sheilagh Kesting, M.A., B.D. — Parish Minister of Overton, Wishaw
9. Rev. Dr. Alan E. Lewis, M.A., B.D., Th.D., Editor of the Report — Lecturer, Department of Systematic Theology, New College, Edinburgh, and Secretary of Panel on Doctrine
10. Rev. Dr. Ian McIntosh, M.A., Th.M., Th.D. — Parish Minister of Old High linked with St. Stephen's, Inverness

Secretary

11. Mrs. Kathleen M. Beveridge, M.A. — Organising Secretary, The Woman's Guild

PREFACE

The main circumstance which led to the preparation of this Report was the use by Mrs. Anne Hepburn, National President of the Woman's Guild of the Church of Scotland, of the titles "God our Mother" and "Dear Mother God" in a prayer at the Annual Meeting of the Guild in April 1982. The Report is to go before the General Assembly of the Church of Scotland in May 1984, and the official response of the Church will then become known.

So intense was the reaction, both negative and positive, to Mrs. Hepburn's prayer, and so great has been the interest, both within Scotland and beyond its borders, in the setting up of a study group to examine the implications of what she said, that the Saint Andrew Press have judged the Report worthy of publication in independent paperback form. They are grateful to the Woman's Guild and to the study group for their permission, and they hope that in this form the Report may attract the attention of many who, whether or not members of the Church of Scotland, are, for a variety of reasons, concerned with the issues which it raises or on which it touches.

It should of course be stressed that at this moment of time the Report carries no authority from the Church. The views it expresses are those solely of the members of the study group which produced it. It is with feelings of inadequacy and not a little apprehension, yet also with the awareness that they are airing matters which ought to be aired, that the members of the group now offer the fruits of their two-year study to a wider public.

April, 1984

1

INTRODUCTION

Origin, Conduct and Goal of the Study

(a) Origin. Following the presentation of the Report of the Woman's Guild to the General Assembly of the Church of Scotland in May, 1982, comment was offered upon the use made by the National President at the Annual Meeting of the Guild some weeks earlier, of a prayer previously published by Rev. Dr. Brian Wren. That prayer had addressed "Our Father", "Lord Jesus", "Holy Spirit", and "Holy Trinity", but also, and controversially, "God our Mother" and "Dear Mother God". It was suggested to the Assembly by the Rev. James L. Weatherhead that the concept of the "Motherhood of God" which this usage implied deserved some study; for it represented a problem which had faced the Church for centuries. He referred to the saying which originated in the Early Fathers that "no-one can have God as Father who does not have the Church as Mother", and also to the view that the Roman Catholic doctrine of the Virgin Mary had developed as some form of compensation for the idea of the Father. More

generally, he suggested that a study of the concept would benefit both the Guild and the General Assembly by providing a useful theological background to other more practical matters relating to the role of men and women in the Church. On his motion the General Assembly passed the following deliverance:

> "The General Assembly invite the Woman's Guild to appoint a small study group to consult with the Panel on Doctrine on the theological implications of the concept of the Motherhood of God, and report to a subsequent General Assembly."

(b) Conduct. This invitation was taken up by the Woman's Guild, and in June, 1982 four of its representatives, namely the National President, two of the Vice-Presidents, and the Organising Secretary, met with the Panel on Doctrine. The Panel agreed with them that this was an important matter for study, which covered a wide range of topics, from the nature of the Deity to the need for sensitivity in liturgical language. It was agreed to set up a joint study group, to be convened and serviced by the Guild, in which representatives of the Panel would try to help the Guild towards fulfilment of its remit. The Panel thereupon appointed four persons to serve on the study group, three men and one woman. Correspondingly the Central Executive of the Guild, in June 1982, appointed six women to

the study group (including the National President, who would be its convener), and this was endorsed by Central Committee in September, 1982. The joint study group has thus consisted of ten people, seven women and three men (with the Guild's Organising Secretary also in attendance), four of the members being ordained.

Following an opening day conference at Carberry Tower in September, 1982, the study group has met at regular intervals over the past two years in the Church offices. Our discussion has, as predicted, ranged widely, and has proved challenging to all of us, not least because of the great diversity of opinion and approach among us. At least one person in the group became a member as a direct result of voicing strong objection to the addressing of God as "Mother"; and this has not proved the sort of committee in which politeness has stifled frank talking, or where a dominant few have silenced the majority. Mercifully, our theological divergence has coincided neither with the female/male or Guild/Panel division of the group, but seems to have reflected fairly accurately the plurality of opinion in the Kirk as a whole on this matter, and differences in society at large about the relations of women and men.

(c) Goal. Given our differences — and the nature of our remit itself — the study group has not attempted to arrive at narrowly-defined proposals about how the Church of the future should speak about its God. Our aim has been to explore, with receptivity but not

without criticism, one dimension of the contemporary theological enterprise. That is the attempt by an increasing number of Christian women and men to understand and speak of God in ways which reflect more fully the female experience of life along with the male. Their efforts have directed our attention to some often neglected aspects of our theological and devotional inheritance from the Christian past. But they have above all sent us back to the Scriptures, compelling us, as befits Christians who stand in the tradition of the Reformers, to wrestle yet again for an understanding of God which is faithful to the old unchanging Word and yet sensitive to the newness of every changing moment. It was inevitable, and appropriate, that we would find such a study of the Scriptures a painful and unsettling process which has left many questions unanswered and some disputes unresolved. But as the General Assembly first invited us to make this study, so we now invite the General Assembly, and the whole Church, to share in the journey of exploration we have made, to overhear some of our conversation — the harmony and the dissent — and to reflect upon the various conclusions we have reached.

The goal must be that in all the variety of fears and hopes, convictions and assumptions, which late twentieth-century Christians bring to such an issue, we may together, women and men, mature in the way we understand, serve and proclaim Jesus Christ, and the One who sent him.

2

BACKGROUND

Seeing the Context

(a) Everyone knows that over the past twenty years Western society has been undergoing a profound transformation in attitudes to, and on the part of, women. They themselves have given identity to what was once "a problem without a name", highlighting a whole range of means — restrictive employment, commercial exploitation, violence — by which through prejudice or custom the equal worth of women was denied, and opportunities for the development of their personhood limited. Undoubtedly a great deal of the impetus for change has come from thoroughly "secular" philosophies; and even those Christians who have most enthusiastically welcomed and benefited from the new freedoms enjoyed by women, will probably have their criticisms of some of the rhetoric, and some of the side-effects, that have accompanied the movement for equality.

Nevertheless, it would be quite impossible to attribute the events of the last two decades wholly to a spirit of the age which is inimical to the gospel. On the contrary Christians have both contributed through their own witness to the changing of social attitudes and practices, and seen the integral relevance of those changes to the Church's own life. An early example of this two-way process, in which the Church has both listened and witnessed to society, was our own denomination's decision in 1968 no longer to bar women from the ordained ministry. The need for much further-reaching steps to be taken in creating "space" for women was recognised in the 1980 Report on "The Role of Men and Women in Church and Society". Likewise, throughout the 1970's many of the world's churches were committed to a theological dialogue in pursuit of "The Community of Women and Men", which culminated in a World Council of Churches (W.C.C.) Consultation on that theme in Sheffield in 1981. Neither merely against sexism, nor merely for women, that envisioned a genuine community, witnessing to a divided society, celebrating the distinctiveness of each person, male and female, yet affirming reciprocity and interdependence, in the faith that women and men are created together in God's image and have been made one in Christ Jesus.

(b) Among the issues which have faced, and internally divided, Christians on this matter of the Community of Women and Men, two stand out in their relevance for this study:

(i) *The Authority and Content of Scripture*. There are some things in the Bible which have appeared to many over the centuries to qualify the absolute equality of women: the derivation of Eve from Adam in one of the creation stories; the maleness of Jesus; Paul's remarks on the subjection and on the silence of women, for example. This poses sharply the question of Scripture's authority. To what extent does the sociological and cultural environment in which a given passage was first written determine the way we interpret its meaning and authoritativeness for us today? And how should we treat passages which in isolation appear to give different answers, to this or any question, from those which Scripture as a whole might be argued to give? In Churches like ours, which are not encumbered, as some are, by the weight of Tradition coupled with that of the Bible (and attesting in this case an exclusively male clergy, for example), our very insistence upon Scripture as the sole written form of God's revelation intensifies the perplexity of those who cannot straightforwardly agree what it is that Scripture "says".

(ii) *The Church's Language*. This leads to another, related issue. Whatever we believe Scripture *means,* the words it uses for the human creatures God has made and redeemed are predominantly male. And that grammatical phenomenon has been carried over into a great deal of the worship — the preaching, prayer and hymnology — of the Church. For many women the fact that God created "man" and has his tabernacle with "men", and that Christ was "born to raise the sons of earth", in no way implies their exclusion from the purposes of God. It simply reflects the nature of some collective nouns in the English language and our custom of referring to one gender as a shorthand for both. For other women these grammatical and linguistic conventions are themselves the product of bias and prejudice, and their continued use in the language of the Church, certainly where obvious alternatives or tolerable circumlocutions are available, is hurtful and offensive. It tends to alienate them not only from the Church, but from the God of whom the Church thus speaks. Where this is a problem for some, must it not — among those who bear one another's burdens — be a problem for all?

(c) These general issues come together very pointedly in the matter before us. For it is clear that Scripture and the language of traditional worship not only use predominantly male language for humanity, but also for God. Especially is it an irremovable datum that our Lord spoke of him who had sent him as *Father* — and invited his disciples to do likewise. Thus the language of male parenthood naturally dominates all Christian attempts to conceive of God and to articulate his relationship both to Jesus and ourselves. In the minds of some, at least, this dominance is reinforced by the sheer fact of the maleness of Jesus, and the faith that it is in the particularity of this *man* that God has revealed himself and assumed human flesh. None of us can avoid the male language of *sonship* for Christ's relationship to God. And even when it is fully recognised that neither the maleness nor the sonship of Christ imply that God is therefore male, some will find here, consciously or unconsciously, additional reasons for *speaking* of God in male terms. Certainly there are many women for whom paternal imagery and male language for God either need not, or cannot, be questioned or added to. When such questioning or addition happens it may be *their* turn to feel alienated. They may feel in no way excluded from a God who happens to be described in terms of a parenting role which biologically is not theirs. They may, after all, enjoy or have enjoyed the best of relationships with their own fathers, or alternatively take comfort in the contrast between the heavenly Father and an absent or unloving earthly parent. Or they may repudiate as irrelevant all such psychological considerations and insist upon the exclusive Fatherhood of God as that which Scripture has revealed and Christ commanded. There are indeed those who believe that even today the language which Christians use of God, and especially *to* God, must be limited to or firmly controlled by the Bible's own vocabulary.

Over against these positions are a very different set of feelings and assumptions. For there are women who strongly express the view — believing they have a right to be heard in a community of love — that an exclusive dependence upon masculine and paternal language for God does indeed have a distancing effect. To them it carries the strong implication that women and mothers do not enjoy quite the same resemblance and relationship to their Maker as do their male counterparts. They point to the fact that the Church which has used paternal language for God has historically been patriarchal in its structures and practices. And they can show that in some cases at least, such patriarchy has been justified on the grounds of a supposed "maleness" of God, as well as of Jesus. Some will feel that, notwithstanding the Church's hurtful misuse of the Fatherhood of God, the authority of the Bible leaves them no freedom to use anything other than its male language. But an opposing view is that Scripture itself may be explored for alternative, or at least complementary, ways to speak of God. Likewise, through the centuries Christian piety and intellectual reflection have added to the vocabulary of the Bible itself, developing a changing language and a more complex set of concepts to express down the ages the unchanging truth and meaning of Scripture. Thus, it is asked, would the Bible's authority be compromised if, expanding upon some admittedly *minority* images in the Scriptures themselves, we were to articulate more precisely in contemporary worship the overwhelming witness of the Bible that women as well as men, mothers as much as fathers, are made in the image and likeness of God?

3

A CRUCIAL ISSUE

Language and God

The preceding section should show something of the context within which the study group's conversations have taken place, and explain briefly how "the motherhood of God" has come to be on the agenda for the contemporary Church at large, and for the Kirk in particular. It takes us directly to the first matter of substance which the group had to deal with, and which we are agreed is a quite crucial issue and a key to many of the problems surrounding the Motherhood of God and to any resolution of them. That is, the nature and function of all human language when applied to God, who by definition transcends human experience.

Despite our varying perspectives and conflicting opinions, we have as a group been dismayed by one major misunderstanding manifest in many of the published reactions to the setting up of this group, and also in some of the material that we have had to consider in the study itself. This is the assumption, quite erroneous in our collective view, that the God of Christian faith has a *gender* and a sexual differentiation, so that to call him "Father" is to attribute to him, as to human fathers, the property of "maleness". The idea that the Father God has a male gender is a major source of confusion and muddled thinking, not least because it is a preconception shared by parties approaching the Fatherhood of God from quite opposite starting-points. There are those in the theological world (not represented on our group), who wish to repudiate "God the Father" precisely because such a God is male, and should be replaced with a God who is female. Yet among those who vigorously defend God's Fatherhood in our own Church, there are clearly many who have always assumed unconsciously, on the basis of that language, that God is "male", if not a "man". And as we have said already, that assumption of a divine, male gender has been used at times to justify forms of church life in which men have appropriated for themselves unequal privileges and prerogatives.

We shall examine in some detail this alleged "maleness" of the Father below, but wish first to make a point of principle concerning all language used in relation to God. Whether we would speak *about* God, in theology, or *to* God, in praise and prayer, the tools at our disposal are unequal to the task. All our images, concepts and statements are inescapably human, finite and creaturely (even, of course, those we find in, or derive from, the Bible — where it is through human words that the Word of God is heard, just as it is in the humanness of Jesus that the Word of God is enfleshed). Our attempt in human language to express something of the inexpressible mystery of God's transcendence is a humble one; a foolish one, if we hope to do so adequately or completely. It has often been said that silence is the first and most appropriate form of human speech before God.

Yet by God's own grace we are not, of course, restricted to such silence. Means are given to us to say and understand something of God's reality and truth. Because we believe that there is some resemblance, a relationship, a correspondence, between human and divine reality, we draw pictures, tell stories, adopt analogies, construct doctrines, confident that while these are only finite expressions of the infinite they are not wholly inappropriate or misleading. The emphasis today upon the use of narrative, parable and metaphor as the most effective, though indirect means, of communicating the incommunicable, only echoes what most theologians have always known about the incompleteness of theological statements, which necessarily fall short of their Object.

How easily, though, we forget this falling short of all our pictures, and all our words. It means that in even the most appropriate and authorised analogy there is something inappropriate, some aspect of the earthly partner in the comparison between our reality and the divine, which does not apply to God, and remains inert, or positively misleading, in the analogy. It might be easier to see the consequence of this for our use of a biologically-conditioned image such as that of a father, if we apply the principle first to an equally familiar but less controversial image, namely that of a shepherd. Scripture encourages us to use this image for God and gives us the best of reasons for thinking that it is a legitimate and appropriate way for human beings to express something true about God's inexpressible nature. Yet we know intuitively, when for example singing "The Lord is My Shepherd", that we are *only* using a metaphor or analogy, which in two respects at least falls short of the reality.

On the one hand, we know that only some characteristics associated with shepherding are actively being brought into play — the shepherd's solicitude, compassion, courage, etc. — and that other elements in the traditional image of the shepherd, such as his carrying a crook, or shearing his sheep, do not really enter into the resemblance with God that is being posited. We know, in other words, that God is not really "a shepherd", any more than we would identify ourselves literally as sheep. But if there are some characteristics of the human shepherd which do not apply when God is so described, we also recognise that there are some characteristics of shepherds which apply *more* in God's case than in the human. This is the great power of analogy in religious contexts: that though we begin with ourselves and apply human images to God, the tables are then turned and the divine reality in its wholeness and truth rebounds upon us, relativising and judging us. Thus while Christ is in one sense not a shepherd at all, in another he is the "Great Shepherd of the Sheep", his solicitude, compassion and courage infinitely transcending any human activity we might literally or metaphorically describe as "shepherding". He is more truly a shepherd than any of us.

Both aspects of the analogical relationship, whereby some of our qualities would be falsely attributed to God, while others are more true of God than of us, are vital to our understanding of what is being affirmed, and what is not, when we call God "Father".

4

RE-AFFIRMING THE TRADITION

The Fatherhood of God

(a) The command. Despite the genuine fears expressed in some quarters of the Church, it has been neither the purpose of this study group, nor the policy of its members, to abandon, change or replace the traditional understanding and address of God as Father. We are interested neither in dropping such language, nor in turning the God of Jesus Christ into a goddess or female deity, still less into a "woman". On the contrary, the centrality and permanence of Jesus' own way of addressing and describing God has been driven home for us as our understanding of its significance has developed. Of course the diversity of Christian approaches to the authority of the Bible, which was described above, has been reflected in our own circle. For some the use of "Father" by Jesus and the rest of the New Testament leaves little or no room for flexibility or discussion on how we ourselves may address God. For others, the

language, conceptuality and doctrine of the Trinity is a simple but important precedent, where the Church developed a vocabulary which was not used by Jesus or the New Testament, yet which we believe to be consistent with, even necessitated by, the Word of God, and which has in fact become a touchstone of orthodoxy.

Yet from either stand-point, that which has been revealed to us in Christ and through the Scriptures is normative and decisive; and this applies above all to what has been given to us to believe and say about God. We cannot but address and approach the God of Jesus Christ as "Our Father". And it is important to be clear about the grounds on which we do so. Naturally our own personal experiences, the memories of family life, or our psychological and emotional make-up enter into, and one way or another affect, our faith and understanding when we encounter our Heavenly Father. Yet Christians do not adopt that language in the first place because we find it "meaningful", but because we have been commanded and permitted to use it. God is our Father not because we have analysed and found illuminating the experience of parenthood or childhood, but because he is the Father of Jesus, who graciously allows his kin to share in that unique Father-Son relationship. Christ is the one who calls, and may rightly call God, "Abba". It is the Spirit of Christ, and not our own inventiveness, who unites us with the Son and liberates us, as his brothers and sisters by adoption, to call God

"Abba" likewise (Mk. 14.36; Rom.8.15; Gal.4.6).

This fact, that the Fatherhood of God is not a product of speculation or psychologising but has the character of "command" and "gift", which may only be heard and received in the context of a faith-relationship to Jesus, is crucial; for it sets the God and Father of Christ radically over against the caricatures which have so often been drawn of him. In other words, although we could not call God Father did we not have some image of the human father, this is the analogy *par excellence* which turns back upon us, judging and showing up the limitations of human fatherhood. God is not confined within the limits of our image of him, but iconoclastically bursts that image, and compels us to learn anew from him the truth about his and all fatherhood. We are not free, therefore, merely to paint our own pictures, and absolutise our own images of God's Fatherhood (for therein lies distortion and caricature), but must hear what the incarnate and written Word of God reveals to us of the Father.

The conviction of the group is that when we do this, two particular false images and caricatures of God the Father are exposed for what they are, with far-reaching implications for the "community of women and men".

(b) The caricatures. (i) Gender. We have already stated our belief, in the face both of those who wish to uphold and those who wish to dispense with a "male" God, that use of a father image does not involve attributing

sexual differentiation to God. This surely is one aspect of human fatherhood which is laid aside or left inert, when following the command of Jesus we affirm an analogy between human fatherhood and God. To do otherwise, assigning to God the biological differences and limitations of human beings, would surely be a form of that idolatrous confusion of Creator with creature described in Romans 1.23-25. There may be quite innocent, unconscious assumptions on the part of many in the Church that, because we call him Father, and because he has revealed himself in a human being of one sex rather than the other, God has a gender. But we believe that a deliberate affirmation of this view seriously threatens the uniqueness and transcendence of the God to whom all our Scriptures witness.

Certainly the designation of the gods as "fathers" is very common in pagan religion, often with biological, sexual connotations, where the ancestor of a nation or tribe is thought to have had a god as his father. The Greek myths told of marriages between the gods of Olympus and mortal women; and the nature religions (including some in the Ancient Near East surrounding the people of Israel), attributed the earth's fertility to its divine impregnation. Perhaps it was precisely to distance itself from such notions that the Old Testament was so cautious about describing Yahweh as Father. When God is Father in the Old Testament it is the special relation of election, discipline and mercy with his chosen people that is referred to. "When Israel was a child I loved him . . . out of Egypt I called my son . . . I led them with cords of compassion" (Hos. 11). This emphasises that not by a natural affinity, let alone biological descent, but by God's own covenantal grace, are the Israelites God's "children". Like all humanity, they are the children not of a divine quasi-sexual or biological *genitor* but of a divine *creator*; and the Old Testament doctrine of creation is uncompromising about the transcendent otherness which separates the Creator from his creatures, even in their likeness. We are made, both male and female, in God's image, and God comforts and pities us both like a father and a mother (see below); but this surely does not indicate a divine sexuality or even a bi-sexuality. Is the Creator not really trans-sexual, or a-sexual, the Lord and Maker of all precisely because he transcends all creatureliness, including the forms and means of creaturely generation?

This transcendence is maintained in the New Testament, where the notion of the divine fatherhood takes centre-stage. The Father is still creator rather than genitor; indeed the whole mystery of the incarnation is that what has become flesh, a creature of human birth, is none other than the Word or Son of the Father, who created and thus transcends everything that "becomes", or is made or born (cf. Jn.1.1–14). Of course, John in particular uses the biological metaphor of "begetting" for the eternal relationship between the Father and the Son; but by describing Christ as the *only*-begotten (1.14; 3.16), he indicates the uniqueness of this relationship, and its difference from any human begetting. So it was that later orthodoxy fought for the divinity of Christ, as creator not creature, by affirming that he was "begotten, not made" (Nicene Creed). That is, they were so far from thinking that the Father was a quasi-male, a human-like, sexual father, that on the contrary they saw the Father's begetting and generation of the Son as the antithesis of biological procreation, and the very guarantee that the Son was eternal and *not* a human creature.

There is, of course, a stretching of human imagery and language to its limits here. And perhaps the bursting-point was reached at a seventh-century Church Council which affirmed that the Son was born *de utero Patris*, "from the womb of the Father". Such a deliberately incongruous and "impossible" use of language shows that the Church Fathers did not suppose that the Father was masculine, but saw that his unique otherness, while embracing the qualities of both father and mother, quite transcended the creatures' separation into male and female.

If then God is without and beyond gender there can be no grounds either for seeking to exchange his maleness for femaleness, or for perpetuating church structures which elevate male members of the community because of their distinctive creation in the image of God. Which brings us directly to the need to correct a second caricature of God the Father.

(ii) Domination. We have already suggested that while it would be false to attribute to God

some of the earthly characteristics of any analogy for the divine, there are some characteristics which we discover to be more true of, or fully present in, God than ourselves. Thus to speak of a divine fatherhood is to confess that all human fatherhood is less than true and complete. All human fathers are, at best, pale reflections and distorted images of the one, true, definitive Father, who is the source and origin of all things, including "fatherhood". (The New Testament itself makes this point about the derivation of human fatherliness from the divine with an untranslatable pun at Eph. 3.14f.: "before the Father (*patera*) from whom every family (all fatherhood?) (*patria*) in heaven and earth is named.")

Does this not mean that instead of imposing upon God's Fatherhood preconceptions and stereotypes about his nature drawn from our own experiences and notions of fatherhood, we must actually let Christ "show us the Father" (Jn. 14. 8ff.; cf. Mt. 11.25ff.), and accept whatever damage that showing does to our presuppositions? Perhaps this applies particularly to our stereotyped connection between fatherhood and domination.

The caricature of God the Father as essentially a *ruler,* a disciplinary and authoritarian being, is commonly drawn and accepted by those who believe that the remote, distant, unfeeling Father of Christian faith must be replaced with a more tender and sympathetic feminine deity. And a similar false image has surely been at work among those who have created and defended an authoritarian, hierarchical and patriarchal Church as a reflection of God's own nature and will. Yet it must be conceded to both forms of this remote and authoritarian caricature that Christian theology at its worst has often presented God in such a fashion.

It is sometimes said today that this presentation of God as impersonal reflects the fact that theology has historically been dominated by men, and that they share a general preference for individuality over relationship, and have a fear of emotion and weakness. However one evaluates such assertions, it is true that the Church has often borrowed its doctrinal categories from various sources in Greek philosophy, and produced an all-powerful, impassible, Absolute deity, more of a Principle or a Cause than a Person. This is deplorable precisely because it so betrays the Bible's own categories. For Scripture, it is men and women, not the principles and causes we detect in the cosmos, who bear a likeness to God.

The Old Testament has its own way of affirming this very un-Greek and personal nature of God: an astonishing range of words and images which assign to God the gamut of human emotions. But this personalising of God comes to its climax in the teaching and history of Jesus and the New Testament's reflections upon him. By having Jesus address God with the novel and scandalous familiarity of *Abba,* and by affirming him as the incarnate and crucified Son, the New Testament declares that God is essentially personal, and moreover that he unites himself to his creatures in the closest of personal relationships, that of parent to off-spring; that instead of keeping his distance he is approachable, accessible and self-giving; and that far from impassible, he is responsive to his children's cries, compassionate upon their misfortunes, forgiving of their waywardness, and identified with their suffering. For the New Testament it is specifically as *Father* that God invites familiarity and intimacy (Gal. 4.6), cherishes and preserves "little ones" (Mt. 18.14) and endures the passionate grief of sonlessness (Rom. 8.32). What more eloquent protest could there be, here in Scripture itself, against the impersonal Absolute of Greek philosophy, with which the Church dallied for too long, and against the remote, invulnerable, patriarchal deity whom both critics and defenders see as the key to the Church's authoritarian past?

(c) The corrective. What an irony it is that something as revolutionary as our Lord's "Abba, Father", should have over the centuries been turned into an instrument of domination and subjection by men who sought and claimed to follow him! In fact we see in the life, teaching and death of Jesus, a heavenly Father quite unrecognisable as the dominant, masterful figure of power portrayed in the caricatures. The gospel carries through a revolutionary challenge to human conventions and concepts, to our understanding and our

behaviour, and does so with the help of a whole series of images which are turned shockingly upside down, and dramatically reinterpreted. Here, for example, is a teacher who tells grown adults that they must become like little children, or even be born again. Here is a master who shows his lordship by stooping before his own disciples to do for them the despicable work of a slave. Here is a priest who presents as a sin-offering of the people, not a lamb bred for slaughter, but his own self: an innocent one made victim. And here is a messiah, expected to liberate his enslaved people with power, instead made captive, and crucified in powerlessness.

So it is too that, whatever domination is associated with and practised by human fathers, it is pity and compassion which characterise the heavenly Father; and though he is a King and Ruler, his kingdom is not of this world, founded on this world's forms of power and justice, but a kingdom for sinners and outcasts and those of lowly status, a kingdom in which the godless are justified. And the King's power is a foolish weakness which uses the nobodies of the world to bring down the somebodies (1 Cor. 1.28).

Of course this revolution in the nature of authority and power, revealed in Christ, does not mean that God is no longer King, Lord and Father. On the contrary, there is laid upon those who believe in him the demand that they become his servants, who acknowledge his authority and do his will. The startling difference between God's authority, kingship, fatherhood, and ours, means that he is not *less* but *more* to be obeyed. It is supremely true of the Father's own Son, and hence true of us who follow the Son, that the Father's will is to be done.

Now perhaps women are entitled to complain that sometimes the Church has created out of this an "ideology of obedience" (D. Sölle), in which they themselves, to a greater extent than men, have been cast as "the specialists in self-denying" (R. R. Ruether), who should particularly embody and display Christian obedience. However, the rectification of this imbalance surely does not lie in women casting off the demands of obedience and discipleship, in favour of power, but in the fresh realisation by us all, and where necessary particularly by men, that service rather than power, obedience rather than independence, is the norm of all Christian living. In a sense it is and should be true of *all* Christians that they are "specialists in self-denying".

Lest it be feared that this simply reinforces for either women or men, ethics and structures which restrict and dehumanise, we should remember yet again the good news of the New Testament about the revolutionary nature of the kingdom of God. For under the lordship of Christ's Father it is the master who becomes the servant, and the servant the master. Captivity is perfect freedom; and in obedience to this King we discover not restriction but liberation. Indeed the Lord so frees those who love him that the master/servant relationship dissolves entirely, and becomes one of friendship (Jn. 15.15). Those who are God's friends do not so much live *under* him as *in* him, sharing in the family oneness of the Father and the Son (Jn. 17.21ff.). And it is precisely because the obedient friends of Christ do form one family that there can be no place among them for grades and distinctions, for some who, *in contrast to others,* specialise either in obedience to God or intimacy with him.

This revelation of what real Fatherhood is like — the very source, rather than the denial, of freedom and community — has often been subject to concealment by an all-too-human Church which finds the way of the cross intolerable. Again and again we have refused to let the Father of Jesus be the model for our thinking and living, as that judges our authoritarianism and independence, and call forth community. And at times orthodoxy has collaborated in this evasion. The Trinity, for example, has often been treated as a unitarian monarchy, and the oneness of God and of his rule has been offered as a justification for the Church's endorsement of earthly monarchs — and for its own hierarchical and patriarchal structures. But as some contemporary theologians are now showing us, this "political and clerical monotheism" (J. Moltmann), is itself a caricature of the Trinity, which is rather a community of mutual interdependence between the three Persons, whose rule creates freedom, and opposes domination and inequality.

C

All this is to say that the Fatherhood of God is its own best corrective to the caricatures made of it. Instead of repudiating belief in and language about God our Father, as a means to making the Church a community in which women enjoy full equality with men, we should on the contrary emphasise the Fatherhood of God all the more, since all that Christ reveals of that Father stands in such clear contradiction of masculine domination. Our group thus whole-heartedly *re-affirms the traditional way of describing and addressing God as Father.* We do so on the understanding that the Christian Church has often drawn from such imagery theological and practical inferences that are incompatible with what the New Testament itself discloses about the nature of God and of the community intended for God's people. The most direct and urgent means of correcting distortions of thought and practice based upon an image of God as a quasi-male, absolute sovereign, is recovery of and return to the Father of Jesus.

5

COMPLEMENTING THE TRADITION

The Motherly Father

Once this re-affirmation has been made, there are, however, further questions to be asked. What are the *implications* of seeing that, some caricatures notwithstanding, God our Father stands quite outside our sexual differentiation as male and female, and radically opposed to those forms of male domination which our stereotypes associate with "masculinity" and "patriarchy"? Is it consistent to say that God is neither "male" nor "masculine" and yet must be exclusively described in terms which are drawn from the biological role and human experience of *men*? Once we are clear, and provided we remain so, that God the Father is not a male, nor masculine, might we be in fact set free to use analogies drawn from the whole range of human experience, of men and of women, of fathers and of mothers, to express what God the Father truly *is*? To use analogies from women's experience of being human would not make God "female" or "feminine" any more than the New Testament analogy of fatherhood makes him male or masculine.

Now our group would not wish to adjudicate in society's contemporary debate about "femininity", *i.e.,* whether in a male-dominated world the goal should be greater recognition and free expression of femininity and female values, or whether the notion of femininity is itself an instrument by which men have defined the roles that women may play. But we are agreed that in all human beings, regardless of their biological determination, there are present and need to be expressed, human qualities which traditional shorthand would describe as both "masculine" and "feminine". And even those of us most opposed to describing God as anything other than Father are keen to point out that in human parenthood, beyond the strictly biological roles which cannot be exchanged, many fathers engage in activities, and exhibit attitudes, which can well be described as "motherly", and vice versa. In fact, for good or ill, we live in an age when one person very often fulfils all the non-biological functions of fathering and mothering single-handedly.

There may be something of importance for our study in this recognition that although human beings are sexually differentiated as either men or women, we are all equally human, with potential for roles and qualities that are both masculine and feminine, both fatherly and motherly. Perhaps it is in this light that we should understand the Bible's use of human parenthood as a central analogy for God. We have argued that in calling God Father, the New Testament does not ascribe to God male gender or biological fatherhood, nor the onesided qualities of masculinity. Surely what is affirmed in the image of the Father are not male, paternal or masculine characteristics particularly or exclusively, but *human* qualities which bear resemblance to, while falling short of, God's truth and wholeness. As "Father", lacking gender and exercising kingly rule and mastery only through vulnerability, tenderness and friendship, is not God revealed as embracing, while utterly transcending, *both* of the distinctive human ways of being persons and parents? Would it be inaccurate or misleading, then, to describe the Father of Jesus actually disclosed in the New Testament, as opposed to the Father of the caricatures we have criticised, as being a most "motherly Father" (J. Moltmann)? Indeed is this a Father whom we could properly characterise *without* using language and imagery — of comfort, compassion, sensitivity, trustworthiness, etc — which rightly or wrongly evoke association with the feminine and the maternal?

If we were agreed that "motherly Father" is a not-misleading description of the God of the New Testament, this further question would arise: should these motherly qualities of the Father be something we simply recognise to be there, but leave largely unarticulated and not referred to — or would it be legitimate actually to use language in the Church which explicitly expressed the fact that the Father we trust and worship is motherly as well as fatherly in nature? Without in any way withdrawing the traditional ways of speaking of God as Father, would it be proper to *complement* that, in some contexts, with language which brought out this fact of the Father's motherliness?

The group all recognise, despite our different interpretations of authority, that the Bible is the decisive norm and guide for the Church's thought and speech. So the key question for us becomes whether Scripture itself provides precedents and material for so complementing the traditional Father God with language which articulates the motherliness of the Father. A considerable proportion of our study has thus been devoted to careful examination of the whole range of Scripture on just this issue: are there *biblical* grounds for speaking of God the Father in analogies and metaphors drawn from the female experiences of human life? Despite the blanket assertions we have heard in some parts of the Church that no such language and imagery exist in Scripture, our own studies have arrived at a significantly different conclusion.

(a) The Old Testament. It could come as something of a surprise to those who assume and repeat that the God of the Old Testament is primarily a God of war, a wrathful and bellicose "Lord of Hosts", to discover there the immensely wide and rich range of references to the love, forgiveness, compassion and pity of God — as befits a Creator whose

essence is not of wrath at all but of covenantal grace and righteousness. What is significant for us is the frequency and beauty with which various forms and aspects of parenthood and parental love are used as similes and metaphors for God's own love.

(i) There is, first, wide use with reference to God of verbs and their associated nouns which specifically mean the love in which both the sexes or both the parents of a family participate. Among the most common of these is *raham,* which is often translated, when in a verbal form, as "to have compassion or mercy", and when a noun as "bowels", "heart", "mercy", etc. The reference in general is to family love or affection (see. *e.g.,* Ps. 51.1; Exod. 33.19; Jer. 31.20). Also commonly used of God (above all in Hosea, but see also Deut. 7.7, and Ps. 146.8), is *ahab,* meaning "love between the sexes". Only most rarely is one sex rather than the other identified when the image is applied to God.

(ii) But what of the images of God which do draw specifically from the personhood, role or attitude of one parent rather than the other? There are a few places where God is addressed as Father (*e.g.,* Isa. 63.16; Jer. 3.19), and several others where he is described as a father (*e.g.,* Jer. 31.9; Mal.1.6). Over the Old Testament as a whole the father image is relatively rare, for reasons discussed above: the need to distinguish the Creator from pagan fertility deities. (Such a "fathering" of nature is explicitly referred to, in repudiation, at Job 38.28 and Jer. 2.27.) Yet sometimes the father image is daringly used to reinforce this "otherness" of the transcendent Creator and Maker (see Isa. 45.10; Mal. 2.10). What is equally striking is the characteristic of fatherhood which is generally highlighted in the analogy with God. Occasionally the father's discipline of his son is identified (Deut. 8.5; Prov. 3.12); but if discipline be thought of as a *paternal* prerogative, then overall the Father of the Old Testament is a notably *maternal* parent. He is likened to the father who pities his children (Ps. 103.13), supports and carries his son (Deut. 1.31), spares his son (Mal. 3.17), and acts as a father to the fatherless (Ps. 68.5). Clearly this divine Father is no more an authoritarian despot than he of the New Testament!

(iii) This brings us to the explicitly feminine and maternal images. Of course by far the most common usage here is of female images to describe not God, but *Israel* as she stands in relation to God — the bride, wife, or daughter of Yahweh (or Jerusalem), prefiguring the Christian concept of the Church as the bride of Christ and the mother of believers. The role played by feminine images in the description of God's people, both in the Bible and in subsequent theology, liturgy and devotion, has been a long and important one. It is a tradition still greatly cherished by many, who would not wish to see a more feminine language for God being paid for by the loss of feminine language for Israel and the Church. Indeed the Bible's regular use of such language to depict Israel might seem to leave relatively little room for manoeuvre to those who would base feminine descriptions of Israel's God on explicit Old Testament precedents.

Nevertheless, a reversal of the normal relation, by which the female or womanly is indeed likened to God, rather than to God's people, is not unknown to the Old Testament. Of particular importance here, perhaps the key text for the whole of our study, is Gen. 1.27 (cf. 5.2): "God created man in his own image, in the image of God he created him; male and female he created them". In itself this text is less significant for what it says about women, or men, or even about God, than for what it says about *humanity* — that we are created by God as persons who are sexually differentiated into men and women, yet are equally created in sexes neither of which can be without, or be superior to, the other. Togetherness and equality in our sexual differences seem to be characteristics of our humanity in God's image. And it is important to note that this text occurs in the Priestly creation story, and thus is distinct from and should not be made dependent upon the second Yahwist account, in which Adam precedes Eve and provides the material out of which she is made. In the simplicity, equilibrium and conjunction of "male and female" at Gen. 1.27 all suggestions of the priority of one sex and the derivativeness of the other are excluded.*

---

*It is true, of course, that the Apostle Paul, adopting a rabbinical form of interpretation, himself derives implications for the behaviour of women from the second creation narrative (1 Cor. 11.7–12; 1 Tim. 2.11–15).Yet it is perhaps significant that his prescriptions for the silence of women, and the veiling of their heads, etc., are based upon the second account rather than the primary, and that in the course of his argument Paul can restore the balance between men and women which is implicit in the first Genesis account but seems to be upset in the second. For he points out that as Eve was made from Adam, so now man is

Only after this equality of the sexes into which our common humanity is differentiated, has been emphasised, would it be legitimate to draw more specific conclusions from Genesis 1.27 concerning the participation of the *female* in the image and likeness of God. Yet against a history in which the Church has often limited to men the privileges of representing and symbolising God, we must do so. It needs saying that whatever it means for human beings to be in the image of God, that mysterious and unspeakable honour is not one whit less enjoyed, or in any way differently, by women compared to men. We must say of every woman, with no more and no less astonishment and boldness than of a man, that she is "like" God, and that her humanity images and resembles the very Creator of all things.

(iv) On the foundation of this affirmation by the Old Testament of likeness between women and God, what other more specific images of female personhood and activity are used to illuminate God's own being and doing? We find a quite remarkable sequence of feminine experiences to which God is likened, ranging from the behaviour of female creatures, to the activities of midwife or nurse, involved at one remove in the birth process, to the whole spectrum of motherhood itself, from conception to suckling to child care. As

born of woman, and that "in the Lord" neither man nor woman is independent of the other (1 Cor. 11.11f.). And that, in turn, echoes Paul's own definitive statement that male and female are one in Christ Jesus (Gal. 3.28). In whatever way he understood the new creation, in which there is neither male nor female, to differ from the first, in which we *are* created male and female, Paul clearly believed Christ to have removed rather than perpetuated any distinctions of rank and order between the sexes. *See also Appendix B.*

instances in this sequence, God is likened to:

the protective mother bird	Isa. 31.5
the mother eagle	Deut 32.11
the midwife	Ps. 22.9
the nurse	Num. 11.12
the mother conceiving	Num. 11.12
the mother pregnant	Isa. 46.3; 49.15
the mother giving birth	Isa. 42.14 (cf. Deut. 32.18)
the mother suckling	Isa. 49.15
the mother quieting	Ps. 131.2
the mother comforting	Isa. 66.13

Even these references, and others like them, are relatively few in number, comprising a minor strand of biblical witness, and none of them amounts to a direct address of God as "Mother". The Old Testament is discriminating in its use of parental imagery, both male and female, for the ways that God takes with Israel and humanity. Yet this genre of metaphor does exist, adding considerable depth, warmth and beauty to the attempts of the Old Testament writers to describe their unnameable God. The presence of these images is all the more striking for the caution which Israel's opposition to nature religion required. Does this relaxation of the Old Testament's own natural and proper reserve set a precedent for us? The question of how, and in what contexts, the Church might utilise and develop this imagery in her own language, we shall postpone until the New Testament and other evidence has been examined. Yet we may make the point already that it can scarcely be described as unbiblical, or without Scriptural precedent, cautiously to make reference to the female way of being human, including the woman's body and its biological functions, in our mumbling efforts to give speech to the unutterable love of our Maker.

(b) The New Testament. By contrast with the Old Testament, though even more, as we have said, with some non-biblical religious and philosophical systems, the dominant feature of the New Testament is the closeness and familiarity it conceives between God and those who have faith in him through Jesus. Scholarly criticism of the gospels establishes as a reliable historical fact the arresting and unprecedented use by Jesus of Nazareth of the term "Abba" for God — a diminutive, familial term for one's earthly father which, though originally a piece of childish talk, had long before Jesus been used among adults also. Taking their cue from this dominical practice, the New Testament writers adopt parenthood as the primary motif for the divine-human relationship — in which God is Father and we are his sons, or children (*e.g., tekna,* a collective for boys and girls). Sometimes human fathers figure in the parables and similes with which Jesus illuminates the nature of God's love and of his kingdom or heavenly rule (*e.g.,* Mt. 21.28ff; Lk. 11.5–13; Lk.

15.11–32). Occasionally, however, women provide him with the appropriate simile (Mt. 13.33; Lk. 15.8); and in one celebrated passage, cherished by many Christian women, Jesus adopts a provocatively maternal image for himself and his own feelings: "O Jerusalem, Jerusalem . . . how often would I have gathered your children together as a hen gathers her brood under her wings, and you would not!" (Mt. 23.37; Lk. 13.34). The free and unaffected manner in which Jesus here associates himself with the protectiveness, and the sorrow, of a mother, must at the very least acquit of blasphemy those who subsequently, with a cautious daring, have spoken of the womanly and motherly qualities of our Lord.

Most of the remaining feminine images as such in the New Testament refer, as so often in the Old Testament, to God's people: to the disciples suffering like a woman in labour at the departure of their Master (Jn. 16.21ff.); to the Church as Christ's bride (Eph. 5.21ff.; Rev. 21.9); or to the apostle who is in travail with the young church (Gal. 4.19), and nursing it to maturity (1 Thess. 2.7). One notable exception — though very difficult to interpret — is the role given to "a woman clothed with the sun" in the dramatic playing out of the last things described in Rev. 12. Whoever she be, the vision places her in close proximity to God, who takes her child to himself (v. 5) and prepares a special place for her (v. 6). Rather than see this as justifying speculation about a divine femininity, it would be safer simply to note once again that Scripture does not rely exclusively on male figures and masculine images to symbolise and illuminate God's lordship and authority over heaven and earth.

This brings us directly to all those concrete deeds in his life and ministry by which Jesus embodied and acted out "the kingdom of God". For if women appear quite rarely in the words that Jesus used concerning the kingdom, they figure with astonishing constancy in those human contacts and relationships through which Jesus dramatically disclosed to his contemporaries the unexpected nature of his Father's kingdom. His friendship with Mary and Martha, his acceptance of Mary Magdalene and of the extravagant and beautiful gestures of love shown by other women of sin (Mk. 14.3ff., Lk.7.36ff.), his protection of the adulteress, his dealings with the woman of Samaria, his appearing first to women on the day of resurrection, and numerous other contacts, have a powerful cumulative effect. Set in a social context of female inferiority and exclusion, they demonstrate unmistakably that women have an equal place wherever God reigns, even if they be treated as unequal in the kingdoms of men. Indeed where that is their lot they have a special place in the Father's kingdom, whose bias is shown by the Son to be towards the weak and the poor.

Again, do not the sensitivity and compassion of Jesus, his acceptance of the instincts, concerns, feelings and gestures shown by the women around him, which so often contrast with the reactions that men had to him, suggest much about the nature of God's ways, as that is embodied and revealed in all that Christ was and did, including his relationships with fellow men and women? Whether or not we consider tenderness, vulnerability, and non-rational sensibilities, to be peculiarly feminine or motherly, it is clear that such, in human terms, are among the characteristics of who and what God is. Certainly there is much that we are compelled to say about the God of the New Testament which we could not say were we restricted to language taken from roles and attributes conventionally seen as "masculine".

(c) Wisdom. Perhaps it is as one more impressive instance of the Bible's refusal to restrict itself to the male sphere in its attempt to articulate the Divine, that we should regard the figure of Wisdom. Wisdom is a central character in a whole genre of late-Old Testament writings and in the inter-testamental literature. For many scholars her presence in the New Testament, though mostly latent, is highly significant also. In Hebrew, "Wisdom" is a feminine noun, as are "Law" and "Spirit". Like these others, though even more personified, Wisdom is a figure closely associated with God: an aspect, expression or agent of the divine activity itself. Most of us in the group would be wary of speculating too far upon the strictly feminine designation of this biblical figure: it would certainly be unwise to build a theological superstructure on a purely grammatical foundation. Even so, there is considerable significance in Scripture's

freedom with such a concept, which not only in its grammar but also in its content (insight, patience, discretion, and deft maturity in relationships), contrasts with the majority of models it uses for God. Though given new meaning when applied to God, ''Judge'', ''King'', ''Governor'', ''Lord'', etc., are as such traditional male roles, and in themselves carry the heavier-handed ''masculine'' connotations of power and control.

This contradiction between ''wisdom'' and power is highlighted in the New Testament. For both Jesus and Paul, God's wisdom (*Sophia* — a feminine noun in Greek also), is revealed precisely in his ''foolish'' preference for the sinful, the outcast and the weak. This revelation happens in the scandalous company Jesus keeps and the scandalous death he dies (Lk. 7.34f.; 1 Cor.1 and 2). If these passages suggest an indirect identity between ''wisdom'' and Christ's own person, there are many who believe that behind the scenes she has greatly and directly influenced some central aspects of the New Testament doctrine of Christ. The view is this: that along with the concept of the eternal and pre-existent Word or Logos, which John's Prologue has being made flesh in Jesus, the early Christians also inherited from late Judaism other pre-existent divine figures, Wisdom notable among them, and that when the New Testament writers elaborated upon the pre-existence of Christ, as one who was always with God before his coming among us (*e.g.* 1 Cor. 8.6; Phil.2.1–11; Col. 1.1–15; Heb. 1.3), it was the language about, and the figure of,

Wisdom which they had in mind, and the enfleshment of God's Wisdom in Jesus of Nazareth that they were affirming. (For a comprehensive discussion of these rather technical matters see J. D. G. Dunn, *Christology in the Making,* ch. VI.)

Now it has been shown possible by contemporary theologians (R. Haughton in *The Passionate God,* most notably), so to write a whole theology of Christ's person and work as to emphasise the embodiment in him of Wisdom as well as of the Word, and to make maximum use of feminine categories and experiences, especially of conception and birth, to describe the fertile and creative abundance of life which God's coming among humanity releases. However "orthodox" in intent, such a use of feminine motifs will strike many in our Church as unconventional and strange, and our group could not unanimously endorse it. What we can, at a minimum, point out, however, is that in coming to understand even something as central to the gospel as the eternal personhood of the Son of God, the authors of the New Testament by no means restricted their range of serviceable concepts to those which were "masculine" in grammar, symbolism or connotation.

6

PROVISIONAL ASSESSMENT

Agreement and Controversy

Other data, relating especially to our inheritance of language and conceptuality from the post-biblical Christian tradition down the centuries, still need to be considered before we can arrive at any conclusions on how the Church may speak of God today. Yet it would be appropriate here to make an assessment of what we have discovered in Scripture itself, and of the choice of inferences which may be drawn from that. By doing so we may underscore the fact that this has not been a speculative study, flirting with neo-paganism, but a serious attempt to ask what is in, and agreeable with, the Word of God.

The preceding discussion sets out our agreed view that while never ever addressing God directly as "Mother", the biblical writings themselves fill out, add to, and complement our Lord's disclosure of God as our Heavenly Father, with a great range of hints and suggestions drawn from one aspect or another of female experience. This spectrum of female characteristics, activities, figures and historical individuals, which we have reviewed, in no way retracts or replaces the Fatherhood of God. Rather it serves to emphasise that this Father neither possesses male gender nor is of such a nature as to be humanly describable only in conventionally masculine terms. When we hear what the Word of God has to say about the Father we discover a fatherhood which embraces and transcends the human differentiations and limitations of role and character. The scriptural data seem therefore to amount to an overall adverbial or adjectival qualification of the Fatherhood of God, which gives expression to his transcending of our divisions. God is not one-sidedly a "father", but a Father who acts "in a maternal way", a King who exercises rule and lordship "with a feminine compassion", etc. And perhaps the shorthand we suggested earlier for all of this is now seen to be well-attested by and fully in keeping with the biblical witness: God as "the motherly Father".

Our whole group is well satisfied that the Bible does warrant such descriptions and qualifications of God's Fatherhood which could legitimately be incorporated into the Church's discourse. Even those most resistant to ever calling God "Mother" wish to emphasise that God is certainly not male, or exclusively paternal, since it is that quite un-biblical misrepresentation which encourages the unacceptable wish to replace God the Father with a female deity. However we have to admit to disagreement among ourselves when the question is raised of going beyond such motherly *descriptions* of God the Father, to a motherly *address* of him.

For some of us this distinction in the use of language is a real and vital one. There is something unique about an approach to God, an encounter in worship and prayer with the living reality of his being. To name and invoke Almighty God is awesome, a privilege not a prerogative; and we can do so only on God's terms, using those names and adopting those forms of address which he himself has willed and authorised. Since Scripture offers no precedent or authorisation for addressing God as Mother, we are not free to invoke God thus either, but are constrained to approach him in the same terms as did our Lord. And in the light of who our Lord is, it is only fitting to address God in terms which reflect the fact that he has ultimately addressed and revealed himself to us in the *man* Jesus.

There are others among us who see this distinction between describing and addressing God much less clearly. For them it is a failing, not a virtue, when the language of theology and that of doxology are kept distinct. Should there not be, they ask, the most natural and imperceptible passage between the two, as we raise up in adoration and confession in personal encounter with God, everything that we have been given to believe and understand about him? The Old Testament addresses God in the imagery of lifeless objects — ''My fortress'', ''My shield'', etc.; may we not do so in terms of human persons made in God's image and likeness? If we have had disclosed to us a Father who cares for us with an unsurpassable sort of love that summons up in Scripture itself metaphors of mother and infant, etc., are we not free to give voice and name to this love when we approach God and praise him for it? For those who take this view, to address God as Mother in such a spirit would be to do nothing inconsistent with what Christ and the Bible have done, but would with gratitude and wonder follow the lead of the Bible, indeed of Jesus himself, in gathering feminine analogies, alongside others, into humanity's humble task of expressing the inexpressible and praising the One beyond all praising.

Thus stands the principal unresolved controversy among us.

7

THE MOTHERLY FATHER IN HISTORY

A Devotional Legacy

(a) Twentieth century Christians do not receive the Biblical record in a vacuum of timelessness. We may believe that in Scripture there is transmitted to us the living and changeless Word of God; yet the way we hear, interpret and respond to its voice is affected by the contemporary make-up of us the receivers, and by the intervening generations of Christian experience and historical development, which constitute the medium through which transmission and reception happen. Our memory of Christian history, and our conscious or unconscious conditioning by past and present cultural variants, inevitably enter into, and must be allowed for in, our approach to the Bible. Yet the effect of being open to the importance of historical factors is not limited to one particular kind of decision about Scripture on specific issues. For example, on the present topic, one person could decide that the biblical witness legitimises approach to

God as Mother and yet feel that the use which has already been made of that conceptuality in the history of Christian devotion constitutes a warning signal for ourselves to proceed only with extreme caution. Someone else might judge the Motherhood of God not to be specifically authorised by the Bible yet be ready to honour and embrace the later history of that concept as an authentic, if so far minor, strand of Christian experience and witness.

Without committing ourselves to either example, and while making, as demonstrated, study of the Bible our principal task, our group has been aware of the importance of the post-biblical tradition. By uncovering, or at least indicating the presence, of one rich vein in the spirituality of the Church's past, we hope, if nothing else, to discredit the myth that those who would today speak of God in the maternal mode are, in their "trendiness", inventing something previously unknown to Christian faith and history.

(b) If an excavation of our inherited foundations yields only a limited and narrow layer on which to build, if we so desire, a feminine and maternal Christian language for God, we might nevertheless be struck by the range of periods and traditions in which that layer appears. As early as Clement of Alexandria (died A.D. *c.*215), a Christian Father was writing:

"God is love,
And for love of us has become woman.
The ineffable being of the Father has out of

> compassion with us become mother.
> By loving, the Father has become woman.''

And if Clement should be suspect as a Christian Gnostic, his use of such feminine imagery has surfaced now and again throughout the history of Greek Orthodox piety, including the fourteenth century mystic and theologian Gregory Palamas:

> "Christ . . . nurses us from his own breast, as a mother, filled with tenderness, does with her babies."

Likewise Russian Orthodoxy has given a very distinctive role to Wisdom, exercising great freedom in developing an identification between Sophia and both Christ and the Spirit.

This latter conception, which has the creative, life-giving, energetic Spirit as the particularly feminine member of the Trinitarian "family" is a not unfamiliar one in Christian art — the religious painting of the Ethiopian Church, for example, commonly represents the Spirit as a mother — yet it also occurs in the radically different milieu of Reformed pietism! Thus the eighteenth-century Moravian, who so strongly influenced both Continental and American pietism, Count von Zinzendorf, could describe the Triune God as:

> "the divine family upon earth, for the Father of our Lord Jesus Christ is our true Father, the Spirit of our Lord Jesus Christ is our true Mother, because the Son of the living God is our true brother."

Within this diversity of tradition, it is of course the medieval West which has contributed most to our historical legacy of maternal approaches to God. A long list of names, some better known than others, could be mentioned here — including Bernard of Clairvaux, Aelred of Rievaulx and Christina of Markyate (all twelfth century), and St Birgitta of Sweden (fourteenth century); but two, a man and a woman, stand out for their influence and accessibility. One of them is St Anselm of Canterbury (eleventh century), whose famous Prayer to St Paul ponders, in the free association of meditation, the meanings of motherhood, including its applicability to Christ and his saving work:

> "And you, Jesus, are you not also a mother?
> Are you not the mother who, like a hen, gathers her chickens under her wings?
> Truly, Lord, you are a mother;
> for both they who are in labour
> and they who are brought forth
> are accepted by you.
>
> . . . .
> For, longing to bear sons into life,
> you tasted of death,
> and by dying you begot them.
> You did this in your own self,
> your servants by your commands and help.
> You as the author, they as the ministers.
> So you, Lord God, are the great mother."

Most familiar, and best loved of all, are the *Revelations of Divine Love,* shown to Julian of

Norwich (fourteenth century). Recounting her visions Julian meditates repeatedly on the motherhood of God, especially in association with God's creativity and our createdness. Thus the Second Person of the Trinity is especially "our Mother" as the one in whom we have been made and who in turn has assumed our own creaturely nature, so that we might be God's children:

> "In Jesus, our true Mother, has our life been grounded through his own uncreated foresight, and the Father's almighty power . . . In taking our nature he restored us to life; and now . . . he feeds and helps us on — just as one would expect the supreme and royal nature of motherhood to act, and the natural needs of childhood to require.
>
> Beautiful and sweet is our heavenly Mother in the sight of our souls; and, in the sight of our heavenly Mother, dear and lovely are the gracious children . . . There is no higher state in this life than that of childhood, because of our inadequate and feeble capacity and intellect, until such time as our gracious Mother shall bring us up to our Father's bliss."

(c) How should we assess this distinctive genre of witness to the motherly Father, the divine "parent" whose creativity, care and nurture is at least as akin to that of human mothers as to that of fathers? Quite personal factors may govern the answer to that question; and as in almost any random selection of Christians there are varying

reactions and evaluations amongst our working party. For some it is a significant feature of this legacy, not necessarily in its favour, that it occurs predominantly within the realm of devotion rather than of doctrinal theology. Something acceptable within the relative freedom of personal piety is not necessarily to be endorsed and incorporated into the rigorous task of clarifying and confessing the faith before the world. The obvious reluctance of theologians of the past generally to admit feminine conceptuality acts as a warning today, some of us believe, against widespread expansion of our own theological models into the realm of the feminine.

But most of us take a different view. Theology is the servant, as well as the conscience, of worship; and the profound spirituality of Christians who have gone before us is a legacy too rich and stimulating for our own public and personal worship to be discarded. That would be narrow, arrogant and self-impoverishing. St Anselm and Dame Julian, and the others, inhabited worlds very different from that of twentieth-century Presbyterians; yet for that very reason their contribution to the one on-going communion of saints is to be treasured. In this instance their contemplation and prayer add not so much to the length of our vocabulary as to the breadth and depth of our understanding of God's infinite being and ineffable love. Those who see the existence and nature of this long historical witness to God's motherhood not as a warning against, but as a stimulus for, the development of our own devotion and liturgy, would point to contemporary instances in which, without compromising the evangelical faith, or even entering the controversial sphere of direct address, the feminine legacy has been movingly incorporated into the present prayer of the Church. Thus, for example, there went out from the W.C.C. Sheffield Consultation on the Community of Women and Men, a Letter which concluded in these terms:

"We invite you to pray with us:
Eternal God, as you created humankind in your image, women and men, male and female, renew us in that image:
God the Holy Spirit, by your strength and love comfort us as those whom a mother comforts:
Lord Jesus Christ, by your death and resurrection, give us the joy of those for whom pain and suffering become, in hope, the fruitful agony of travail:
God, the holy Trinity, grant that we may together enter into new life, your promised rest of achievement and fulfilment — world without end. Amen."

(d) There remains to be considered one crucial objection and impediment to any appropriation of the Motherly Father into the piety, liturgy and worship of our own Church. As we have acknowledged, it is above all from the medieval church that this inheritance has come to us. And this clearly confirms in the minds of many an assumption that there is something peculiarly Roman Catholic about

"the Motherhood of God". This has been expressed regularly in published criticisms of this present study — which occasionally have taken the association further by identifying "the Motherhood of God" with Roman Catholic veneration of the Virgin Mary as "the Mother of God".

Our group unanimously calls for clear-headedness and sensitivity in this matter, and wishes to point out forcefully the absolute distinction between considering "motherly" analogies for God, and ascribing to Mary the title Mother of God. *To be a mother, and to have a mother are not one and the same!* And we believe that the biblical and historical data reviewed above allow us to decide for or against the use of feminine metaphors for God in total independence both of the mother of Jesus and of the Queen of Heaven of traditional Roman piety and dogma. (In origin, of course, the title Mother of God affirms the divinity of the child whom Mary bore, rather than any quasi-divinity of that child's mother.) It would in fact be inappropriate for us to pursue a full analysis of Mariology. That phenomenon is relevant here only to the extent that the concept of the Motherhood of God has been perceived as a by-product of, or first step towards, the worship of Mary, or as something upon which any Church opposed to such worship must also, in logic or prudence, turn its back. We thus make the following points:

(i) We affirm the impossibility of treating

Mary as an object of worship or adoration, as one who co-operates with Christ in our redemption or in his intercession with the Father. Nor can we see that the biblical and Reformed doctrine of salvation through the grace of Christ alone is intended as, or may be interpreted as, implying some difference in the standing of men and women respectively before God. That God's saving grace was enfleshed in a man, Jesus, and that neither the woman Mary nor the Church, the ''feminine'' Bride of Christ, co-operate in his mediation, does not, as is sometimes suggested, signify a bias in Reformed theology in favour of men, the active agents, or against women, the passive recipients. Whatever judgment is contained in *sola gratia* is shared by all of humanity, regardless of sex. But much more important is the positive gospel of *sola gratia,* that in Christ the humanity of women and men, equally and in unity, is affirmed, renewed and fulfilled. One cannot say that our sexuality is irrelevant to salvation, since it is as distinct individuals, and thus as persons each with our own sexuality and gender, that we are created and redeemed. But our sexuality makes us different from each other only within the prevenient oneness of our humanity; and it is in the commonness of that humanity, and not differently in our sexuality, that we are both estranged from and reconciled to God. The group can therefore endorse neither the use of a passive Mary to subjugate women, as more essentially recipient than men, nor the use of a sinless Mary to elevate women, as more inherently pure and obedient than men.

(ii) When, however, the dogmas and devotion surrounding the Virgin Mary have been subjected to the criticism of Reformed theology, the question remains whether the phenomenon of Mariolatry has anything to teach a Reformed church. It is impossible to give a simple answer, psychological, sociological or theological, to the question *why* the veneration of Mary arose and has persisted. But as was suggested to the General Assembly at the time of this study's inception, one aspect of the answer surely lies with some form of feminine "compensation" in a highly patriarchal church. Of course the question now asked by many Roman Catholic women especially, is "who are the agents of this compensation?" Does the piety which surrounds the Virgin represent a valid expression of the feminine — the distinctive spirituality of women breaking through the male hierarchical structures and finding by this means a release, articulation and recognition which is denied women in the more formal channels of worship and ministry? Or are women the victims rather than the exponents of compensation — the male system itself glorifying one woman in order to appease the many, and to foster among them the Marian ideal of female submission to the male Master?

The common denominator between these explanations is a church structure which denies full equality and space to women. And whether in protest against subordination, or as a means of perpetuating it, Mariolatry is a clear example of unacceptable doctrine resulting from and reinforcing unsupportable practice. As such it is a warning of what may happen anywhere, when the full integration of women into the spiritual and organisational life of the Church is impeded. In the imposition of such inequality, or in the resistance to it, distortion and imbalance are inevitable, and the ultimate victim is the liberating truth of the gospel itself. As stated before, the fundamental concern of our group is that *ours* should be a Church in which, in the interdependence and distinctiveness of the sexes, the humanity of all is recognised, affirmed, and given full and equal expression. Only such a community, free of bias and polarisation, of authoritarianism and rebellion, can hold to and embody the gospel of Christ, whose truth sets us free and whose peace makes us one.

(iii) It seems entirely possible to our group that once we have set aside the unbiblical role of the Queen of Heaven, the actual historical figure of Mary, the mother of Jesus, has a real contribution to the greater recognition and freedom of women in our own Church. Though the Motherhood of God stands or falls without reference to her, she does stand out among the many women whose relationships with Jesus helped him to reveal to us the loving, motherly nature of his Father's rule. Of course it is a striking fact that, far from idealising or elevating her, Jesus in the gospels can speak with surprising asperity to his mother (Lk 2.49; Jn. 2.4), and go out of his way to subordinate his physical relationship with her and his family to those spiritual bonds which make all people of faith and obedience his "brother and sister and mother" (Mt. 12.46–50; Lk.11.27f.; cf. Jn. 19.25ff.).

Yet does not this sheer ordinariness of Mary in the gospels in fact set us free to recognise that about her which is extraordinary and significant, without fear of idolatry? As the first person to say "yes" to Jesus, as the one chosen and willing to bear his person in the body as others are called to bear his image spiritually, she is a prototype of Christian faith, and in that sense at least a representative of all of us in the Church. In a sense her femaleness is incidental: biologically required for the role she is given, but not theologically significant. In Mary's humble responsiveness to the Spirit, and exultant willingness to be used by God, we see the true faith of a human being, not that of a woman exclusively. And yet it is not inconsequential, especially for women, that this unique human role in the incarnation is given to and accepted by a woman — and one more indictment of much church history which has disparaged the gifts of women and restricted their leadership.

There are those who believe that the reluctance of a Reformed church to give recognition to Mary betrays a fear of femininity as much as a fear of Rome, and that we will not embody a genuinely free and equal "community of women and men" until we have come to terms with our anti-Roman inhibitions and found an evangelical freedom to remember with particular honour and

E

respect one character in the gospel story, as good and as fallen and as ordinary as any, yet chosen to be the mother of our Lord and therefore "blessed among women".

8

CONCLUSIONS

Discrimination and Opportunity

The inception of this study at the invitation of the General Assembly was a cause of considerable disquiet in some quarters, which has never totally ceased through the lifetime of the group. Negative reactions to the study have ranged (sometimes within the one critic!), from its dismissal as a triviality, a waste of time and expense, to the fear that it is a serious threat to the gospel, likely to undermine the faith of church-members and Guildswomen. Many, of course, shared the view of the General Assembly, and welcomed an open-minded, free examination of the issues. This spectrum of opinion has, as indicated, been reflected in the composition and conversation of the study group itself. Yet the group as a whole trusts and believes that the foregoing report will lay to rest many of the fears and misunderstandings which have surrounded our discussions. It has, for example, been our intention to show that consideration of motherly language for God does not mean:

(i) *A surrender to secularism.* The group

members, like all Christians, differ in their evaluations of the changes in our society often summed up as "Women's Liberation"; yet we all see it as an indicative of the Christian gospel, not simply an imperative of secular social revolution, that women and men, in all the variety of their differences, are equal before God and in the community of his people. To ask questions about how those who have been created equal may speak about their creator is a privilege and responsibility of Christians, quite independent of trends and values in outside society.

(ii) *A return to paganism.* The Report demonstrates that, whatever an individual's conclusions and decisions, the question of the "motherhood of God" can be asked and answered as an issue of biblical exegesis and interpretation, governed by the criterion of what is true to Christ and his Word, and to the exclusion of any unbiblical neo-pagan goddess religion.

(iii) *A flirting with Roman Catholicism.* Representatives of many Christian traditions besides the medieval forerunners of "Roman Catholicism" have used feminine language, especially in prayer and devotion, to express some aspects of God's being and Christ's salvation. We have set out above our reasons for believing that the concept of the Motherhood of God is to be affirmed or denied independently of any approach to the mother of the incarnate Son of God comparable to that of traditional Roman piety.

(iv) *An abandonment of the Father.* It has

been taken for granted by the study group that no change, or rejection, or substitution of the Church's traditional language for God is implied when the question of God's motherhood is raised. The only possibility under review is that of complementing the traditional language in ways consistent with Scripture's richness and variety. The controversy among us is whether such an enrichment of our language could extend to the mode of address, or must be restricted to that which we say *about* God.

Although we hope that these and other fears are shown by our Report to be unfounded, we do naturally recognise that anything new, perhaps especially in an age when much that is familiar and cherished is disappearing, rouses suspicion and in fact demands circumspection. Objectively speaking, as we have shown, the use of feminine imagery to describe and invoke the God of the Bible is not new (any more than the Church of Scotland is the first denomination, even among Reformed churches of this nation, to consider its implications — cf. for example the Ecumenical Report of the Congregational Union of Scotland, 1982). Still, though not new in itself, the concept of the Motherhood of God is new to many of *us*, which psychologically amounts to the same thing. And the new, inevitably strange and disturbing possibility this group has been invited by the Church to consider is that, along with many other changes affecting the relation and role of women and men in present church and society, we might enrich our prayer, our hymnody, our preaching, perhaps, and formal liturgy, and certainly our private meditations, by a greater use of feminine language and imagery for all that God is and does.

Our conclusions are these:

That the God whom we have called, and must still call "Father" is not a male deity, nor a God whose character is that of a "masculine" authoritarian ruler, writ large. The kingly power of his lordship is that kind of weak and foolish power revealed in the cross of Christ. His love is infused with that sort of tenderness which we glimpse in the relationships of this Jesus with the "inferior" women of his day. It is a love which Jesus himself, and many Old Testament writers, discover on occasion to be best conveyed with metaphors drawn from female and maternal experience. Nor is the Bible's freedom with such imagery surprising, since its central affirmation where men and women are concerned is that we are created equally and together in a mysterious resemblance to God, and that the disharmonies and inequalities which sin intrudes upon the sexes have been overcome in Christ. All human language is inherently inadequate for the task of expressing and addressing God. There are, in any human-divine analogy, elements which are at best inert, at worst quite wrong. And because of the danger of misinterpretations which would compromise the Creator's transcendence, the Biblical writers treat "parental" language about God with caution.

That applies especially to the Old Testament, and to motherly language even more than fatherly. We can scarcely be less discriminating. Since the Church has on the whole taken advantage of the Bible's careful freedom with the feminine much more readily in the unrestrained arena of personal devotion than in the stricter confines of formal theology, the need for caution has been doubly impressed upon some. Of course neither our Report, nor any measure of acceptance which the General Assembly might give to it, would impose upon anyone any requirement to use in any context whatsoever, language they deemed incautious, unbiblical or unauthorised. As explained, some of us feel strongly the obligation to restrict our language of address to that which has been directly authorised by our Lord and his Word. Indeed the final conclusion of a small number of our group, whose voice has an important and equal right to be heard, is that feminine analogies for God, though present in the Bible, *form a secondary witness compared with the New Testament's dominant testimony to the Fatherhood of God. Although they acknowledge gratefully the motherly qualities of this Father, they believe that to call God "Mother" would be illegitimate, and cause hurt.*

On the other hand, the remainder of our group, while reaffirming the need for discrimination and sensitivity, do wish to draw attention to the plight of those people who feel alienated and distanced from their Maker and Saviour by the exclusive use in the Church of male language for a God known not to be male. These members ask if the "community of women and men" would not be brought a small step nearer if the Church were to take more seriously this particular pain, which is felt deeply by some. They have come to the conclusion that real, if limited, opportunities have been offered by the biblical witnesses themselves, for anyone who so wishes, to speak a language which some earlier brothers and sisters in the faith have spoken. *For they believe that they have heard it said in the Word of God that the Father of our Lord Jesus Christ, the Maker of us all, resembles, though he far transcends, everything that is best in the female way of being human and the human way of being motherly.*

APPENDICES

A. BIBLICAL PASSAGES CONSIDERED BY THE STUDY GROUP

1. God as Father

Exod 4.22–23
Deut. 1.31; 8.5; 32.6,18,19–20
2 Sam. 7.14 (of the king)
Job 38.28
Pss. 2.7 (of the king); 27.10; 68.5; 89.26 (of the king); 103.13–14
Prov. 3.12
Isa. 1.2,4; 9.6 (Messiah as); 30.1,9; 45.10; 63.16
Jer. 2.26–28; 3.14,19; 31.9,20
Hos. 11.1–9
Mal. 1.6; 2.10; 3.17
Mt. 5.16; 5.43–48 (Lk. 6.27–36); 6.7–15 (Lk. 11.1–4); 6.25–33 (Lk. 12.22–31); 7.7–11 (Lk. 11.5–13); 10.26–33 (Lk. 12.2–9); 11.25–27 (Lk. 10.21–22); 18.14; 21.28–32; 23.9; 24.36; 26.39,42
Mk. 14.36
Lk. 2.49; 12.32; 15.11–32; 23.34
Jn. 1.14–18; 3.16–18; 5.17–23; 6.32; 8.19,39–47; 10.14–18,29–30,37–38; 13.1,3; 14.1–11; 15.9–10; 17 *passim;* 20.17
Rom. 8.15–17,29,32
1 Cor. 8.5–6; 15.24
2 Cor. 1.3–5
Gal. 4.6–7
Eph. 2.17–18; 3.14–15; 4.4–7
Heb. 1.5–9; 2.10–11; 12.9
Jas. 1.17,27
1 Pet. 1.17–19
1 Jn. 1.1–3; 2.1; 4.9
Rev. 1.5–6

2. The Weakness of God

Isa. 52.13–53.12; 63.9
Mt. 8.19–22 (Lk. 9.57–62); 21.4–5; 26.51–54
Mk. 8.31–38 (Mt. 16.21–27; Lk. 9.22–26); 9.33–37 (Mt. 18.1–5; Lk. 9.46–48); 10.13–16 (Mt. 19.13–15; Lk. 18.15–17); 10.35–45 (Mt. 20.20–28; Lk. 22.22–27)
Lk. 1.46–55; 24.25–27
Jn. 3.14–17; 11.33–35; 13.1–5; 15.12–17; 18.36
Rom. 8.17,26,32

1 Cor. 1.17–31; 9.19–23; 13
2 Cor. 4.5–11; 6.3–10; 8.9; 11.16–30; 12.5–10
Gal. 2.20
Phil. 2.1–11
Heb. 2.10–18; 4.14–16; 12.1–3
1 Pet. 2.18–25
1 Jn. 4.7–12

3. God as Mother

Gen. 1.2 (God's Spirit)
Exod. 19.4
Num. 11.12
Deut. 32.11,18
Job 38.29
Pss. 17.8; 22.9–10 (as midwife); 27.10; 36.7; 91.4; 131.1–3
Isa. 31.5; 42.14; 46.3–4; 49.13,15; 66.13
Jer. 31.15–22
Mt. 23.37 (Lk. 13.34) (Jesus as); cf. Lk. 19.41–42

4. God/Jesus as Husband/Bridegroom and Israel/the Church as his Wife/Bride

Song of S. *passim* (on the traditional allegorizing interpretation)
Isa. 49.18; 50.1; 54.5–7; 61.10; 62.4–5
Jer. 2.20,32; 3.1,6,8,20
Ezek. 16 *passim;* 23 *passim*
Hos. 1–3 *passim*
Mt. 22.1–14; 25.1–13
Mk. 2.19–20 (Mt. 9.15; Lk. 5.34–35)
1 Cor. 6.15–17
2 Cor. 11.2–3
Eph. 5.22–32
Rev. 12.1–6; 19.7–9; 21.2,9; 22.17

Israel/the Church as Mother

Isa. 47.8–9; 49.19–21; 50.1; 54.1; 60.4; 66.7–9,10–12
Jer. 4.31; 6.26; 8.19–9.1; 31.15–17
Lam. 4.3
Joel 2.23
Mt. 2.17–18
Jn. 16.20–22
Gal. 4.19 (the apostle); 4.26–27; 6.16
1 Thess. 2.7 (the apostle as nurse)
2 Jn. vs.1

5. Biblical words for Love

Two Hebrew verbs which, with their associated nouns, are frequently used of God, have close links with many of the passages considered above:

(a) *raham* = family, perhaps basically maternal love (cf. *rehem* "womb"), though it is used just as often in "fatherly" passages; usually translated "(have) compassion, mercy, pity"

(b) *ahab* = basically love between the sexes; usually translated "love".

Both are very warm and emotional words but, though sometimes present, it would be a mistake to look for traces of their basic meanings every time they occur in the Hebrew Bible.

Examples:

(a) Exod. 33.19; 2 Sam. 24.14; Pss. 51.1; 77.9; 102.13; 103.13; Isa. 49.13,15; 54.7,8; 63.15–16; Jer. 31.20; Hos. 1.6; 2.1,23; 14.3

(b) Deut. 4.37; 7.7,8; 2 Sam. 12.24; Ps. 146.8; Prov. 3.12; 15.17; Song of S. 8.6–7 and *passim*; Isa. 43.4; 63.9; Jer. 31.3; Hos. 3.1; 11.1,4; 14.4.

The N.T. equivalents of these words do not have the same basic connotations in Greek (indeed *eros* "(sexual) love" does not occur in the Greek N.T). These connotations can therefore only be read in via the Semitic background of the N.T.

6. "Lady" Wisdom

Job 28
Prov. 1.20–33; 3.13–20; 8; 9.1–6
Mt. 11.25–26
Mk. 6.2–6
Lk. 2.40,52; 7.31–35; 11.49
Acts 6.3,10
1 Cor. 1–2 *passim;* 3.18–19; 8:6
2 Cor. 1.12
Eph. 1.9–10; 3.8–12
Col. 1.1–20; 2.1–3,20–23
Heb. 1.3
Jas. 3.13–18

7. Mary, the mother of Jesus

Isa. 7.14 (where the Hebrew word means simply "young woman" and not necessarily "virgin")

Mt. 1.18–25; 10.37–39 (Lk. 14.25–27)
Mk. 3.31–35 (Mt. 12.46–50; Lk. 8.19–21); 6.1–6 (Mt. 13.53–58; Lk. 4.16–30)
Lk. 1–2 *passim*; 11.27–28
Jn. 2.1–11; 19.25–27
Acts 1.14
Gal. 4.4

B. BIBLICAL ATTITUDES TO WOMEN

Although not, strictly speaking, within its remit, the Study Group could not avoid facing up to this issue because of the way in which, subtly or unsubtly, people's views on the "Motherhood of God" are coloured by it. Apart from Genesis, only N.T. passages were considered in detail.

Gen. 1.26–28; 2–3 *passim;* 5.1–2
Mt. 5.27–28; 21.31–32; 28.9–11
Mk. 7.24–30 (Mt. 15.21–28); 12.41–44 (Lk. 21.1–4); 15.40–47 (Mt. 27.55–61; Lk. 23.50–56); 16.1–8 (Mt. 28.1–8; Lk. 24.1–11)
Lk. 7.11–15; 8.1–3; 10.38–42; 15.8–10; 24.22–24
Jn. 4.7–42; 8.1–11; 11.1–46; 12.1–8; 19.25; 20.1–18
Acts 18.26
Rom. 16 *passim*
1 Cor. 6.12–20; 7.1–5; 11.2–16; 14.33–35
2 Cor. 11.2–3
Gal. 3.26–29
Eph. 5.21–33
Phil. 4.2–3
Col. 3.18–19
1 Tim. 2.8–15; 3.1–5; 5.1–16
2 Tim. 3.6–7
Tit. 2.1–8
Heb. 11.31
Jas. 2.25
1 Pet. 3.1–7
Rev. 2.20–23

There was no argument in the Group about the positive (and indeed, for its age, revolutionary) thrust of the Bible's teaching on women as evidenced in texts like Gen. 1.26–28 and Gal. 3.28 and, above all, by Jesus' own attitude to them. Its members were also at one in regretting that many traditional interpretations (humorous or serious) of the Adam and Eve story have been insidiously biased against women. The chief disagreement among them centred on those late N.T. passages which, sometimes in noble, sometimes in harsh language, counsel a subordinate role for women in marriage and in the Church.

Most members felt that such an attitude to women stood in some contrast to, and could not claim equal weight with, that seen in Jesus' own example, the declaration of Paul that there is neither male nor female in Christ, and the church situations reflected at Acts 18.26 and Romans 16, which mention women in teaching offices alongside men. The late, controversial passages could not be simply ignored, but they did have to be understood as reflecting their social and cultural background, and perhaps the disciplinary problems which faced the apostles at the time of writing. No more than with the N.T. references to slavery, could they be *directly* applied to the very different social circumstances of today. Another factor weighing with the majority was Paul's rabbinic methods of interpreting O.T. texts (methods well known from Jewish sources like the Talmud); this, when properly appreciated, ought to make us who are not Jews wary of following them too straightforwardly.

A minority, while not unaware of the force of these arguments, did not consider that they warranted setting aside or subordinating a significant strand of Biblical witness. Unpleasant as some of the texts may sound, they contain within them insights valid for every age. They should not be understood as departures from the Bible's positive teaching about women, but as attempts *within that positive teaching* to define the different but complementary roles of men and women in a Christian society. Properly interpreted, they protect rather than demean the position of women, and in no way contradict testimony elsewhere in Scripture to the equality of women with men in both creation and redemption. Within that equality, they encourage co-operation between men and women rather than the removal of role differences. Indeed the traditional ordering of the sexes, which reflects and has been influenced by just such texts as these, has served Church and society well, and stood the test of time. It should not be lightly overturned.

It should be noted that the majority and minority in this tangential discussion were substantially, but not wholly, the same as in the main discussion.